CLASS ACTS

Confession Sessions

Marie T. Morreale

SCHOLASTIC INC.

NEW YORK TORONTO LONDON AUCKLAND SYDNEY
MEXICO CITY NEW DELHI HONG KONG

With much love to Patsy O'Sullivan.

She was the coolest.

Front Cover: (top, left to right) Ilpo Musto/ LFI London Features; Steve Granitz/Retna; Malluk/Repfoto; (bottom, left to right) Peter Kramer/Galella; Lisa Rose/Globe Photos; Jeff Slocomb/Corbis Outline.

Page 2: Eddie Garcia/Shooting Star; Page 4: Gilbert Flores/Celebrity Photo; Page 5: (left) Jeff Slocomb/Corbis Outline; Page 5: (right) Paul Fenton/Shooting Star; Page 6: (left and right) Paul Fenton/Shooting Star; Page 7: (left) Lisa Rose/Globe Photos; Page 7: (top and bottom right; Page 8: Gilbert Flores/Celebrity Photo; Page 9: Adrian Lewis/Hutchins Photo Agency; Page 10: (left) Walter Weissman/Globe Photos; Page 10: (right) Joseph Galea; Page 11: Joseph Galea; Page 12: (left to right) Roce/Shooting Star; Fitzroy Barrett/Globe Photos; Nina Prommer/Globe Photos; Rita Black/Shooting Star; Page 13: (left) Bill Davila/Retna; (right) Walter McBride/Retna; Page 14: Andrew Eccles/Corbis Outline; Page 15: (left) Andrew Eccles/Corbis Outline; (right) Fitzroy Barrett/Globe Photos; Page 16: Sandra Johnson/Retna; Page 17: Marc Royce/Corbis Outline; Page 18: (left) Janet Gough/Celebrity Photo; (right) Kathy Hutchins/Hutchins Photo Agency; Page 19: (left to right) Tom Rodriguez/Globe Photos; James M. Kelly/Globe Photos; Gilbert Flores/Celebrity Photo; Page 20: (left) Paul Fenton/Shooting Star; (right) Jill Johnson/Hutchins Photo Agency; Page 21: (left to right) Theo Kingma/Shooting Star; Bernhard Kuhmstedt/Retna; Patrick Giradino/Shooting Star; Page 24: Steve Granitz/Retna; Page 25: (left) John Kelly/Retna; (right) Steve Granitz/Retna; Page 26: (left) Steve Granitz/Retna; (right) Lisa Rose/Globe Photos; Page 27: Steve Granitz/Retna; Page 28: John Spellman/Retna; Page 30: (left) Armando Gallo/Retna; (right) Jim Cooper/Retna; Page 31: (left) Gilbert Flores/Celebrity Photo; (right) John Spellman/Retna; Page 34: (left) John Spellman/Retna; (right) Paul Fenton/Shooting Star; Page 35: (left to right) Milan Ryba/Globe Photos; Miranda Shen/Celebrity Photo; Steve Granitz/Retna; Page 36: (left and right) Lisa Rose/Globe Photos; Page 37: Fitzroy Barrett/Globe Photos; Page 38: Jill Johnson/Hutchins Photo Agency; Page 39: (left) Kelly Jordan/Globe Photos; (right) Steve Granitz/Retna; Page 40: Pablo Alfaro; Page 41: Kathy Hutchins/Hutchins Photo Agency; Page 42: (top) Mark Allan/Globe Photos; (bottom) Henny Garfunkel/Retna; Page 43: Theo Kingma/Shooting Star; Page 44: Milan Ryba/Globe Photos; Page 45: (top) Steve Granitz/Retna; (bottom) United Press International; Page 46: Lisa Rose/Globe Photos; Page 47: Paul Fenton/Shooting Star; Page 48: The WB.

ISBN 0-439-21027-5

Jason Behr

CONTENTS

Confession Sessions of the Stars
Uh . . . Thanks For Sharing!

A mortifying moment. A totally embarrassing sitch. A trauma-rama. Please tell me this isn't happening!

Call 'em what you will, we've ALL so been there. (And will again, no doubt!)

What are they, exactly?

Well, how about . . . your mother running after you on the school bus — with your brown bag lunch . . . your braces popping out in class when you're at the blackboard . . . any kind of rip in anything you're wearing when other people are eyewitnessing . . . a snort-drenched laugh . . . a stain in the most obvious of places — to everyone else but you . . . tripping over your own feet at the school dance.

Had enough? Well, all righty then!

Mortifying moments are equal opportunity cringe-makers!

As the fictional, but wise Cher Horowitz from *Clueless* says, "In every cloud there's a bunch of that silver stuff." Translation: The cool part about those to-die-from moments is that no one is safe! Not the captain of the football squad, the lead in the school drama, the coolest teacher, hippest big brother, superstar sister, or smooth idol.

Which brings you to this book.

Freddie Prinze, Jr.

Britney Spears

Justin Timberlake

As you're about to find out, today's top stars of the movies, TV, sports, and music have all been players in the "open-mouth-insert-foot" game — just like you. Think Justin Timberlake of 'N Sync is immune? Wait'll you hear about the time he broke his finger onstage and howled in pain . . . mid-song! Think Britney's never gotten off the bus at humiliation station? Then you never heard her talk about the time a mean old teacher singled her out in front of the entire class. Think Freddie Prinze, Jr., is protected from drama-trauma? Check out his memories of being dissed by his girlfriend at a school dance.

Their stories will make you giggle, gag, and mostly be glad that what happened to them didn't happen to you!

Boy Bands Blushing

They're hotties, complete cuties who make total request music. Check out some real-life disasters that happened to the guys in your favorite boy bands that they surely did NOT request!

'N Sync

Justin Timberlake: "I broke my thumb onstage about two and a half years ago at an open-air festival in Mainz, Germany. It was hot out, so they were spraying the audience with water, and some of it got on the stage. When I tried to do this dance move where we slide on one foot, I slipped and smacked my right thumb. It just [went] pop! It was during our last song, so I kept going. I walked around and held the mike with my left hand, and I was like, [singing] 'Hey — ow! — tearin' up my thumb!'"

Chris Kirkpatrick: "I was doing a magazine photo shoot. I was driving around on a motor scooter. I went right through this bush, and didn't realize how thick it was. I thought I was gonna come busting out of it. But as I came out, I had moss and leaves all over, surrounding my head so I couldn't see. I went to put on the brake, but my hand pushed the gas. So I got up, and I'm riding a wheelie with moss all over my head! Then the bike started to shake and the front wheel went back down. I did a flip-over — and landed on my face in front of everyone."

Justin Timberlake

6

Chris Kirkpatrick

Lance Bass: "[On our recent tour] Joey stuck a Superman doll behind a speaker, and I tripped on it. I was like, 'Joey, leave your good luck charms at home!'"

Joey Fatone: "We were on tour in this small town, and the only room service you could get was pizza. Anyway, it was really late at night, and I was so sleepy that I actually fell asleep on the box after the delivery guy left it on the table next to the bed. The other guys [were] laughing [at me when they] woke me up!"

JC Chasez: "This thing [a charm on a chain] around my neck — I've had on for about five or six years. I don't take it off. . . . One time it fell off onstage and I flipped out. [It was] the last song of the show, I freaked. I lost my mind. The charm fell off, almost . . . I was shaking, like really, really messed up about it. . . . It was embarrassing later on."

[Note: Luckily, one of 'N Sync's bodyguards found it on the floor.]

Lance Bass

Joey Fantone

JC Chasez

Backstreet Boys

Howie Dorough: "Once, when we were doing a concert in Germany, there was a part where AJ was [working up] the crowd and Nicky didn't realize that I was right behind him. He swung his arm out and I kinda fell offstage."

Kevin Richardson: "I lost my pants onstage during the very first show of [the Millennium] tour! We had zippers on the side of them and mine just completely unzipped on both sides. The crowd enjoyed it, though."

Brian Littrell: "When I was sixteen, I used to work at Long John Silver's, a fast-food place in my hometown. One day, the company bigwigs came in to check up on us. I was in the back, frying the fish as always, trying to be extra careful. But I accidentally knocked over a huge vat of batter, and it came pouring out and headed straight for one of them! I tried to stop it, but it was too late. It got all over his suit pants and totally covered his shoes. I took my apron off — I thought, 'That's it, I'm fired.' But my boss just said, 'Go get a mop.'"

AJ McLean: "We were asked to wear these strange outfits for a Spanish magazine and they wanted me to dress up like the Riddler from Batman. They gave me this skintight, green body-stocking which was [awful]. The photographer took a few shots before I decided it [wasn't working]!"

Nick Carter: "I was playing basketball with the rest of the BSB and [another group] Solid Harmoni€. I wasn't doing well, and [in frustration] I bounced the ball really hard against a wall. It ricocheted straight back, hitting AJ's mom on the head! She shouted at me in front of everyone like I was just some little kid!"

Backstreet Boys

Nick Carter   Howie Dorough   Kevin Richardson
   Brian Littrell   AJ McLean

98°

Justin Jeffre: "We do a routine with mike stands and one time it completely fell apart on me in the middle of a song!"

Jeff Timmons: "My most embarrassing moment? I have a plethora of them. I'm always falling and looking like a jerk. I'm very uncoordinated."

Drew Lachey: "In Bangkok, I got food poisoning. I was in [a hotel] lobby getting measured for a suit. The lobby was filled with fans. I felt my stomach flip, and I remember running to the bathroom and losing everything. When I opened the door, thirty people took my picture — with drool dripping down my face! It was so [bad] that my bandmates got embarrassed!"

Nick Lachey: "My most embarrassing onstage incident? One time I had to get up on a chair, and it flew out from under me. I landed on my back!"

Youngstown

David "DC" Yeager: "I was leaving a friend's house and trying to act all cool, but I wasn't paying attention to where I was going and I walked right into a pole. It was really embarrassing."

James Dallas: "I was once out dancing at a club and trying all these intricate moves. Somehow, I smacked my head and knocked myself out!"

Sammy Lopez: "I totally tripped while walking up onto the stage one time!"

98°

Jeff Timmons

Drew Lachey

Nick Lachey   Justin Jeffre

LFO

Rich Cronin: "I was in Germany, and we were onstage, and somehow, my mike fell out of my hand, and flew into the crowd, and I was stuck up onstage without a mike for a very long time."

Brad Fischetti: "In school we used to play this game — Two for Flinching. One of your friends would [fake a punch] and if you flinched, they got to hit you two times. One time I turned around in science class, and this guy was trying to play the game with me. It was right after we watched some movie about death or something, and when he accidentally punched me, I thought I was dying. He didn't do it on purpose, [but] they took me away in a wheelchair to the nurse. My mom had to come from work, and I thought she'd be compassionate, but she was like, 'Get over here! Let's go home!' I was like, 'Mom, I just got punched in the nose!'"

Devin Lima: "When I was in high school, in gym class they used to call me Vanilla Ice. As a joke, they threw cake — vanilla ice-cream cake — at me, and I got in trouble for that. I had to clean the mess. But, still it was sort of funny."

Brad Fischetti

Rich Cronin

Rich Cronin

Devin Lima

LFO

Bryan McFadden   Kian Egan

Mark Freehily   Nicky Byrne   Shane Filan

Westlife

Bryan McFadden: "I stole a football from a Gaelic football team in Dublin. I was about eleven and I had to throw the balls back, but my auntie's house was right behind the goal and I knocked it into [her] garden so that I could keep it. My dad went mad and made me give it back!"

Kian Egan: "My most embarrassing moment? It had to be my first job — I was a kisser-gram. I only did it once or twice when I was seventeen. I wore this silly outfit [and I would have to go] to a girl's house on her birthday, read her a poem and kiss her."

Mark Freehily: "[One time when I was home] I was walking into my bedroom. I tripped and whacked my head on the mattress. It couldn't have been dangerous. Glad no one else saw it!"

Nicky Byrne: "I went to an all-boys school and I was in the choir. One day we went to the girls' school next door to sing with them. One of my mates had a rubber snake with him. It was long, green, and really lifelike! Anyway, while they were singing, I threw the snake at the choir girls. They were all screaming and running around. [The embarrassing thing] was that I got caught!"

Shane Filan: "Once I really embarrassed myself. I had these big Speedo shorts on and I didn't tie them up properly. I jumped in [the pool] and they ballooned up and slipped off. So I was desperately trying to stay under the water until I [could get] them back up!"

School Daze Disasters

Faye Tozer (*Steps*): "When I was at school I sneezed on purpose as this boy did the high jump so he couldn't concentrate. He fell over and looked really silly. I got detention from my gym teacher."

Selma Blair (*Zoe . . .*): "My first prom wasn't too much fun. I wore this fussy white dress my mother picked out — it looked like a big bunch of toilet paper."

Scott Vickaryous (*Get Real*): "I was a small guy in high school, and there was a joke about whether I could fit in a locker. I got into one, and my friends locked the door on me and went to class! I actually fit, but I was squished. A teacher came by half an hour later and got me out."

Toni Braxton: "One day I didn't do my homework, so I pretended I was sick [and they sent my mom to pick me up]. She arrived wearing sweatpants, white socks, high-heeled black shoes, and a silk green shirt!"

Faye Tozer

Toni Braxton

Scott Vickaryous

Winona Ryder

Michelle Williams

High School Memories to Forget

- **Winona Ryder** says because she had such short hair, some school bullies mistook her for a guy and beat her up!
- **Jennifer Love Hewitt** must have gone to the same school as Winona — except her tormentors were girls. She recalls some jealous-jennies once poured Coke all over her!
- **Claire Danes** may be an Ivy Leaguer now — she goes to Yale — but she did fail one test three times — her driving test. She got her license on the fourth try.
- When **Michelle Williams** of *Dawson's Creek* was thirteen, she costarred in the TV series *Lassie*. "Every time I walked across the school yard, people would go, 'Woof! Woof! Did you play the dog?'"
- In elementary school, **Brandy** says the girls used to tease her because she was so skinny. "They pulled my hair and tried to jump me after school," she recalls.

Carson Daly

Mama Didn't Lie

Full Name: Carson Jones Daly
Birthdate: June 22, 1973
Birthplace: Santa Monica, CA
Parents: Mom, Patti;
stepdad, Richard Caruso
(Carson's biological father died
when Carson was five)
Sibling: Older sister, Quinn
Early Career Goal: To be a professional golfer
First Showbiz Job: DJ internship at KCM, a radio station in Palm Springs, CA
Career Break: Carson was hired as a DJ by two more California radio stations and,
in 1996, MTV offered him a job as a VJ
Current Job: Host of MTV's most popular show, *Total Request Live*

When Carson was still a radio DJ, he started interviewing a number of music celebrities. As a matter of fact, he was the first American reporter to interview Canadian-born singer Alanis Morissette. Was he cool, calm, and collected? No. Admits Carson of his celeb meet-'n'-greet job back then — and even now that he's "the man" at MTV:

"If you don't get nervous, it means you don't care. But I don't get nervous about the guests [who are] coming on because of their celebrity status. I get nervous 'cause I'm about to go on national TV and people have the assumption that I am one hundred percent prepared, confident, and know exactly what I'm doing. When in reality, I don't. When the camera goes on, I just pretend like I'm talking to a room full of my friends."

Showstoppers

Of course, even among friends there are open-mouth-insert-foot times, and Carson recalls a few of them:

"Embarrassing moment? We were taping, and I didn't know we were live because we sometimes rehearse. Somebody forgot to say at three o'clock, 'We're on!' I was just talking off the top of my head and making jokes. Thankfully, I didn't say anything too bad."

That incident may have caused Carson a slight blush, but the next turned him beet-red!

"My most embarrassing moment definitely was when my mom was a guest on MTV's *12 Angry Moms.* She was sitting next to Puff Daddy's mom, Busta Rhymes' mom, and Notorious B.I.G.'s mom, telling them about me running around as a little kid, pulling my pants down, and stuff like that. I ran into Puffy later and he wouldn't stop teasing me!"

Britney Spears

Singled Out (And not in a good way!)

Birthdate: December 2, 1981
Birthplace: Kentwood, LA
Parents: Dad, Jamie; mom, Lynne
Siblings: Bryan, 22, and Jamie-Lynn, nine
Early Career Goal: To be a singer
First Showbiz Job: *Ruthless*, a play in New York City
Career Break: Disney Channel's *New Mickey Mouse Club*
Current Job: Pop singer

She may be the current reigning princess of pop, but eighteen-year-old Britney remembers there were times in her life when she just wanted to pull the covers over her head and disappear!

One of Brit's very first "most embarrassing moments" was when she was a mere tot of six. Even today she recalls the awful feeling of being unfairly singled out in front of her classmates: "When I was in the first grade, I was mortified because I had the meanest teacher. I was, like, the sweetest student, [but] I talked when she told me not to. But that was because somebody asked me a question and I answered it. She put me on detention! Is that not mean? I had to sit on the steps for recess and I cried the whole time. Mean old teacher!"

Another time, Britney felt the heat of the unwanted spotlight was when she was on her school track team. Britney was at a meet and all set to race. "I was, like, standing there and I was getting all pumped up to go," she says. "[The start of the race] was so fast — the official [shot the starter's] gun, and I didn't hear it. I just stood there and looked blank. He did it so fast. I was like, 'Oh well.' I was really embarrassed." Oops!

Even with super-success, there have been times Britney wishes had never happened — like the time she tripped onstage with 'N Sync. A fan had thrown a cupcake to one of the guys, and when Britney made her move to come out onstage, she stepped right on it, and took a flying slip right in front of everyone!

But that incident isn't on the top of Britney's "Most Mortifying Moments" list. No way! "My worst moment so far in the business happened [in concert] in Fort Wayne, Indiana," Britney says. "I was singing and . . . my headset and microphone were connected to this [receiver] that was taped on my body, and it all just fell off. I just put it back on really quickly, but it was so embarrassing. Thank goodness it was during my last song. If it had been at the beginning, I would have died."

Love Notes

Blushes Caused by Crushes

Love never is easy. Some of Hollywood's hottest stars remember just how hard it can be!

Crush Crisis

Jerry O'Connell (*Scream 2*): "[I asked out] Neve Campbell more than a dozen times when we were teenagers and we worked together [on TV's *My Secret Identity*]. She didn't return any of my phone calls. It was kind of sweet justice coming back to play her boyfriend in *Scream 2*."

Scott Wolf (*Party of 5*): "When I have to go up to a girl and ask her out — that makes me blush. [Once] I went up to a really nice-looking girl to talk, hoping to ask her out, and all of a sudden she introduces me to her boyfriend. Yes, I blushed."

Majandra Delfino (*Roswell*): "I was at a WB press event with Brendan Fehr, [who plays] Michael on *Roswell*. Anyway, I have this very big crush on an actor who will remain nameless. As he walked in the room, Brendan goes, 'Oooh, he's hot!' Then the actor came up and gave me a kiss hello, and Brendan started making kissing noises! He so knows [about my crush]."

Scott Wolf

Majandra Delfino

Nicky Byrne (Westlife): "I get really shy around girls. I think it's because I never know what to talk about and I worry that I'm going to get laughed at. It doesn't stop me talking to someone I like, though. I just hope I don't say anything wrong!"

Lucy Liu (*Ally McBeal, Charlie's Angels*): "When I was in high school, I had a really big crush on this guy. We were walking home together one day, and when I got to my house I figured out that my skirt had been tucked into the top of my underwear the whole time."

Dating Dos and Don'ts — Okay, Mostly Don'ts

Grant Hill (Detroit Pistons): "The first time I went out on a date [with wife, Tamia], I forgot my wallet. I went to a nice restaurant and ordered, like, appetizers, salad, food, and the whole nine yards — and then I reached in my pocket and there was no wallet! That was pretty embarrassing, but luckily she bailed me out."

Leelee Sobieski (*Here on Earth*): "Once, [I had this righteous argument] with a guy I really liked — right in the middle of it, my brace pinged out of my mouth and hit him in the face. He started laughing really hard — it was awful!"

Lucy Liu

Grant Hill

Leelee Sobieski

19

Freddie Prinze, Jr.

Topher Grace

Freddie Prinze, Jr., remembers a moment he would like to forget: "My date Rebecca and I got in this argument at the Winter Ball dance [in high school]. She was dancing with another guy, so I started dancing with another girl. We made up and I said, 'I'm glad we could work things out,' and she was like, 'Nah, I don't think so. We should break up.' I had no ride home, so I had to wait until she was ready to go while she danced with other guys."

Topher Grace (*That '70s Show*) is still shocked by a classmate's reaction to his asking for a date: "I went up to ask a girl to the Christmas dance. She laughed at me, and then said, 'Oh, you're serious.'"

Jordana Brewster (*The '60s*) remembers that her first foray into dating was awful: "When I was about fourteen, I couldn't go on dates because I'd get so nervous. I used to throw up and I couldn't eat for days. I remember having to dump two different guys I really liked because they were making me physically sick. Isn't that weird? They asked, 'Why are you dumping me?' And I was like, 'You make me sick — literally.'"

Meredith Monroe (*Dawson's Creek*) still blushes with this tale: "I asked this guy out after meeting him only a few times. I couldn't remember his name, but I knew it started with an 'S.' So I said, 'Hi, Scott. I don't know if you remember me, but I'm . . .' That's when he said, 'Meredith, yeah, I know who you are. But my name is Steve, not Scott.' I think I disappeared into my coat. But luckily he said he'd go out with me."

Making That First Impression

Rachael Leigh Cook (*She's All That*): "A friend and I were going on a bike ride, and she had gone back to her house to get something. As I was waiting for her, this cute guy was going door-to-door collecting for charity. He said, 'Hey, how's it going?' I said hi — and put my foot on [my bike] pedal and just tipped right over. He laughed at me. I was most definitely not laughing."

Mila Kunis (*That '70s Show*): "I was at the movies, and when I left the rest room, I had toilet paper sticking out of my panty hose. My friends decided it would be a fun joke not to tell me. When we came out of the theater, we saw this cute guy from my school. He looked at me and was like, 'You have paper sticking out of your butt.' I turned tomato-red!"

Eddie Cibrian (*Third Watch*): "I played football when I was a high school freshman, and I had a crush on one of the cheerleaders. One afternoon, she was watching us practice, and my eyes were more on her than on the game. I ran down the field right into the goalpost and blacked out. She noticed all right — so did the entire team and the school nurse."

Rachael Leigh Cook

Mila Kunis

Meredith Monroe

Christina Aguilera

Fame — The Pain Game

Full Name: Christina Aguilera
Birthdate: December 18, 1980
Birthplace: Staten Island, NY
Parents: Mom, Shelly Kearns; stepfather James Kearns; father, Fausto Aguilera
Siblings: Sister, Rachel, 13; stepbrother, Casey, 16; stepsister, Stephanie, 13; half brother, Michael, 3
Early Career Goal: To be a singer
First Showbiz Job: A contestant on *Star Search* — or as Christina says, "a *Star Search* loser."
Career Break: Disney Channel's *New Mickey Mouse Club*
Current Job: Pop singer

Today Christina Aguilera is a superstar who jumps onto jet planes and is whisked away to all corners of the earth. Being on the move is something she's used to. Before her sixth birthday, Christina and her family lived in New York, Texas, New Jersey, and even Japan, because her dad was in the army.

When her parents split, Christina was six years old. Her mom, Shelly, moved her two young daughters, Christina and Rachel, back to her childhood home in Rochester, PA, to live with her mother, Delcie Fidler. In 1992, Shelly married James Kearns, a paramedic. Though she was settled, Christina was still affected by her early on-the-go lifestyle. "I always envied people who had best friends they've known since they were little, because I've never had that," she explains. "I'd have to keep picking up and moving."

On the Outside Looking In

Christina had always felt a bit alienated when it came to friends because she moved around so much and wasn't able to make lasting relationships. Things intensified when she decided to follow her dream of becoming a singer. Christina performed at local events, and when she was eight the talented tyke competed on the TV show *Star Search*. Her loss on the show was something she could handle, but the reaction of some hometown folk wasn't — they seemed jealous that Christina had been on TV, even though she lost.

"As soon as *Star Search* happened, a lot of my mom's old friends, other parents, wouldn't talk to us anymore," Christina recalls. "Sometimes teachers made it difficult — [for example] I would be out with the flu, and I would return to school and the teachers would be like, 'Oh, she wasn't out sick; she was out singing somewhere.'"

Worse was the effect her early "fame" and schedule had on her friendships. It seemed many of the kids at school were jealous of her outside interests. Christina's mom told *Teen People*: "Christina would cry every time her name got in the local paper. We had threats of slashed tires and her getting beat up. She would be late to school because I had to time [when we were] leaving the house so that there wasn't enough time for them to do things to her. She started having nightmares."

Her friends and supporters were few and far between. Remembers Christina, "I would make one friend and these girls would steal [her] away. It was tough."

Eventually, the family moved and Christina transferred to a different school. But that helped only a little bit. Christina was still pursuing her career, and there were times she spent entire semesters being home-schooled. When she did return to the classroom, she didn't fit in.

Dating was usually a disaster, too. "The worst dates [were] with guys too scared to talk to me. Back in my hometown, I was sort of a local celebrity, so guys would be a little intimidated of what I did. It would be kind of sad, because all I wanted to do was have a laugh and get to know them, and they were too scared to even talk to me!"

TV Series Stars' Secret Soap Operas

Check out some of your TV faves most embarrassing moments—on and off screen!

Melissa Joan Hart (*Sabrina, the Teenage Witch*; Sabrina): "We had to do a scene on *Sabrina* where it was raining inside in the hallway, and we could only do it once because I had to be soaking wet. I had to run off set, and when I went to stop all I saw were my feet right in front of me. It was like a cartoon! My feet came up, and then I fell. I landed so hard, and all the cameramen were right there."

Lindsay Sloane (*Sabrina, the Teenage Witch*; Vallerie): "I had an audition for a McDonald's commercial when I was thirteen or fourteen. We were supposed to be eating ice cream and telling jokes. I laughed so hard that the ice cream shot right out of my nose! I thought my career was over, but I ended up getting the commercial. They said I was the most real of the group."

Melissa Joan Hart

Seth Green (*Buffy the Vampire Slayer; Oz*): "I know what it's like to feel like a loser. True rejection is when you're standing on the kickball field, and people are picking teams, and you're the last chosen."

Alyson Hannigan (*Buffy the Vampire Slayer; Willow*): "I went on one of those spinning rides at an amusement park, and it made me so nauseous I decided to take it easy and go on the merry-go-round. Then I started concentrating on the fact that I was still spinning. Sure, I was going slow, but I was still spinning. I jumped off the merry-go-round and threw up in a trash can. This little kid came up to me and said, 'Ha-ha! You threw up on the merry-go-round!'"

Alyson Hannigan

Seth Green

David Boreanaz

Christopher Gorham

David Boreanaz: (*Angel;* Angel) "I was trying to get into a [private] high school and had to meet with one of the headmasters. My pants ripped right down the seat, and then I had to do the interview. Needless to say, I didn't get in."

Christopher Gorham (*Popular;* Harrison): "My senior prom was awful. I was only going with a friend because I didn't have a date. I got food poisoning, and I spent the entire evening in the bathroom."

Leslie Bibb (*Popular;* Brooke): "I felt like a big geek in high school and I still feel like a big geek. . . . Popularity creates a false sense of fulfillment. Sure, you get to go to all of the cool parties, since you're 'in,' you get all of those perks. But those perks come with pressure to conform."

When Leslie was sixteen she won a modeling contest sponsored by Oprah Winfrey. "When something like that happens, you think, 'Wow! I'm cool!' But I ended up feeling my best and my worst. Girls at my school were very mean to me. They would say, 'Why'd you win? You're not pretty!' Winning that contest may have opened a lot of doors for me, but it sure didn't stop me from getting stood up for my junior prom!"

Ben Foster (*Freaks and Geeks;* Sam Weir): "I understand isolation very well. Growing up in a small town in Iowa and being the token actor doesn't really go over well, unless you're also on the football team or you're wearing your cutoff Axl Rose T-shirt."

David Gallagher (*7th Heaven;* Simon): "I caught the garter at a wedding, and had to put it [on] this sixteen-year-old girl that I didn't know. I was like, ten. It was not pretty. It was a girl from the other side of the family who I've never seen in my life, and I had to stick this thing on her leg. I was just not happy. It was pretty embarrassing."

Rider Strong (*Boy Meets World;* Shawn): "[On] my first day guest starring on *The Practice,* my call time was at seven A.M. I set my alarm, but I forgot to flick up the button that actually turns it on. I woke up to the phone ringing from the set. I cut myself trying to shave fast, then jumped in my car and hit stopped traffic. The entire cast and crew waited two and a half hours for me. After doing something like that, it's so hard to prove that you're a professional."

Leslie Bibb

Frankie Muniz

Full Name: Francisco Muniz
Birthdate: December 5, 1985
Birthplace: Ridgewood, NJ
Parents: Denise and Frank Muniz
Siblings: Sister, Christina, 15
Early Career Goal: To be a professional golfer
First Showbiz Job: Playing Tiny Tim in *A Christmas Carol* at the Raleigh Memorial Theater in North Carolina when he was eight years old
Career Break: TV movie *To Dance With Olivia*
Current Job: Star of FOX-TV's *Malcolm in the Middle*, and film *My Dog Skip*

Bullied Boy

The 14-year-old star of *Malcolm in the Middle* seems to be taking all the success of his series in stride. "I don't see myself as different from other kids," he says. And he means it. Though he's been acting since he was just starting grade school, Frankie has never made too much of it. He even admits that his friends back home in New Jersey haven't seen a lot of his work. "A lot of them didn't believe me about [*Malcolm in the Middle*] until they started seeing the ads," he laughs.

Though Frankie loves his TV character, he is the first to proclaim, "I don't share that much with Malcolm because I don't come from a dysfunctional family. My family is very great, and I'm not a genius."

Well, Frankie's IQ may not be Malcolm-high — 165 — but he does admit, "When I was in school, I was getting straight As."

Smart Boy vs. Smart Alecks

But what does he mean, "When I was in school"? Like many child actors Frankie is home-schooled. His mom teaches him both on the set of Malcolm and at home when the show is on hiatus. Because of the young actor's schedule, it's easier that way.

However, Frankie has strong memories of being in a regular classroom — not all of them happy. Back then, like Malcolm, he often was picked on by school bullies.

"They picked on me because I'm really short (4'11") for my age and stuff," Frankie explains without a hint of self-pity. He deals with it as a fact of life, accepting that there will always be people who have to make themselves feel bigger and better by trying to put other people down. The irony is that the people the bullies tease are often brighter, more talented, and eventually more successful than their tormentors.

Frankie has learned the easiest way for him to deal with these insecure bullies is to laugh at them. "I just come back with something really stupid, I guess, to make them feel that it's not so cool to [bully someone]," he says.

Hmmm, seems like a pretty intelligent answer to the problem — maybe Frankie shares a lot more with Malcolm than he thinks!

Your Faves' Secret Fears and Hang-ups

They Confide What Makes Them Feel All Icky Inside!

Hang Ups

Heather Locklear (*Spin City*): "I used to worry that my legs looked way too thin, like little chicken bones. Now that I'm older, I couldn't care less. I've learned the most effective thing I can do when I'm worried about the way I look is to accept my life and stop nitpicking my every flaw."

Alicia Silverstone (*Clueless*): "Sometimes it seems weird that people could think of me as being pretty, because a lot of times I feel like this ugly, fat blimp. To get rid of that feeling, I try to remind myself it's what I have on the inside that counts most. There are so many more important things for me to worry about than if my thighs are too big or if my hair looks nice enough."

Heather Locklear

Alicia Silverstone

Will Smith

Tori Spelling

Will Smith (*Wild Wild West*): "See these huge ears? They were always like little satellites. I'm surprised I don't get cable in my brain with these things. In high school I thought I just looked awful, and the other kids teased me about looking like Dumbo. Of course, there's nothing you can do. Eventually, girls started thinking my ears were kinda cute, so things can turn around."

Tori Spelling (*Beverly Hills, 90210*): "Going through [adolescence] in public is like having your high school yearbook televised. I would love to erase having platinum hair."

Jennifer Lopez: "I have always hated my rear end. It's not exactly fat, but Latin women have round butts. No matter how much I work out, it stays round. I've been in movies where the directors are like, 'How are we going to hide her butt?' I guess I've finally learned to deal with it. You can't change some things — that's just the way your body is."

Hanson

Humiliation Horrors

Zac   Taylor   Ike

With fourteen year-old Zac around, older brothers Isaac and Taylor have a "library" full of embarrassing moments! Known as the "wacky" brother, Zac has definitely caused a stir almost everywhere Hanson goes. There was the time that he jumped down into the audience and pulled a girl up onstage because she was too embarrassed to go up herself. And then there's the favorite question of reporters, "What are your worst habits?" Zac jumps in before either Ike or Tay can say anything and starts blabbering about gross bodily functions! But the fact is that it isn't only zany Zac who's found himself red-faced. No way!

Pssst, It's Taylor!

Check it! Once, when Hanson was over in the United Kingdom on their Middle of Nowhere world tour, a young girl had won a contest to be in the "Where's the Love" video. In the initial script, she was supposed to kiss Taylor, and she was so excited she kept telling everyone on the set, "Oh my God, I'm gonna kiss Taylor!" Well, according to some on-the-set insiders, Taylor got cold feet and nixed the lipsmack scene because he was so embarrassed by all the hoopla!

But Taylor doesn't have to be in front of the cameras to be embarrassed. There's the classic story of the time he went to a McDonald's and was waiting on line — like any normal person — to order food. "All of a sudden there was whispering going up and down the line and people were saying, 'Hanson. . . Taylor,'" he recalls. "No one said anything to me, they just whispered and I was just standing there. In the end, I got my food and ran out."

Kisses Aren't Always Sweet

Of course, Ike has had his "I wish I wasn't here" moments, too. One time, when Hanson was playing the Hershey Amusement Park in Pennsylvania, fans started throwing kisses to the guys — Hershey's Kisses. "I didn't ever think of Hershey's kisses as lethal weapons," Ike laughs, but he found out the hard way. He spent half the show dodging them, and just when he thought he'd made it through the barrage of candy, he got hit in the head with a bunch! Embarrassing? You bet — how can you say "Ow!" because you were hit by a kiss?

Zac Attack

And then there's Zac. We don't have enough pages to list all the times Zac has rated on the embarrassment Richter scale, but here's a classic. When Zac first started playing the drums onstage, he was still a little guy; he had to sit on a trunk so he could reach the drums. During one song, Zac got so into it, he leaned backward . . . and fell over! Being a pro, Zac knew the show must go on, so he climbed right back up and kept playing, but his red face could have given Rudolph's red nose a lesson or two!

Blues Blasters

Your Faves' Top Tips on Turning a Frown Upside Down

Drew Lachey of 98° sometimes uses comfort food to chase the blues away. "My grandmother makes me 'Surprise Weiner Buns.' They're hot dog buns with a bunch of stuff like cheese and hot dogs ground up and put inside. It sounds really nasty, but I was raised on them."

Jennifer Love Hewitt sings away her blue mood. "A lot of people don't know that I'm a singer. So, if I'm feeling down, I love to sing. I love everything from show tunes to Shawn Colvin. It's an instant mood fixer."

Jada Pinkett Smith reaches out to others. "I go to schools and talk to underprivileged kids. I don't care how many problems you have in your life, that is instant joy. You see their faces looking up at you and smiling, and suddenly it all becomes so clear why we are here."

Drew Lachey

Jennifer Love Hewitt

L.A. Lakers' Shaquille O'Neal just "escapes" in his car. "When I get upset, I jump into the car and get lost. Driving around, I listen to my [sound] system, pumped up. In the process of getting myself found again, whatever was bothering me has been forgotten."

Houston Comets' Sheryl Swoopes pampers herself. "When I feel bad, I like to go shopping! I also like to get a pedicure, manicure, and massage!"

Adam Sandler (*Big Daddy*) gives himself a pep talk. "I talk myself out of feeling blue. I always say, 'Okay, this is bad, but it's not as bad as . . . [fill in the blank].'"

Jonathan Jackson (*Deep End of the Ocean*) gives himself a dose of U2. "Good music [fixes] a bad mood. Probably something off the *Joshua Tree* CD or a little 'Mysterious Ways' off *Achtung, Baby*."

Brandy (*Moesha*) soothes away stress and blues. "I go to the sauna and sweat [it out]. I come out feeling like a whole new person with refreshed skin."

Shaquille O'Neal

Sheryl Swoopes

Adam Sandler

The Best Advice I Ever Got . . . or Gave

Even superstars have moments of insecurity when they seek out words of wisdom and encouragement from those they trust the most.

Words to Live By

Tiger Woods (professional golfer)
Advisor: His father, Earl Woods
Advice: "Pop would remind me how important it is to prepare for life's challenges so that I could face them confidently. But when he would tell me, 'Son, you get out of [golf] what you put into it,' I understood exactly what he meant: That no one is going to give you anything in life unless you work hard and bust your rear end."

Brandy (*Moesha*)
Advisor: Her mom, Sonja Norwood
Advice: "One thing my mom told me a long time ago that has stuck with me is to stay [out of the way of bad situations] and keep moving. I try to remember that as often as possible."

Ashton Kutcher (*That '70s Show*)
Advisor: His dad, Larry
Advice: "My dad told me, 'Do it right the first time or don't do it at all.'"

Tiger Woods

Brandy

Neve Campbell

Neve Campbell (*Party of 5*)

Advisor: Actor, Robert DeNiro

Advice: "I was worried about taking a role that was different from anything I'd ever done. But Robert DeNiro [whom she'd met at a dinner] said to me, 'You're young. Do it.' That was pretty great advice."

Nicky Byrne (Westlife)

Advisor: The group's manager, Ronan

Advice: "He told us, 'Be nice to everyone when you're on the way up, then they'll be nice to you on the way down.' All bands have a down side eventually, so you mustn't get big-headed, just be polite. Not false, but friendly."

Mila Kunis (*That '70s Show*)

Advisor: Oprah Winfrey

Advice: "Oprah said something like, 'Know where you're going or otherwise you'll never end up where you want to be.'"

Words of Wisdom

Monica on Boyfriends Who Cheat!

The singer follows her own example from her number one hit video with Brandy, "The Boy Is Mine." She insists: "If I caught my boyfriend messing around behind my back, he'd be out of my life in no time. I don't need a boy bad enough to put up with his player ways."

Kate Winslet on Weighty Matters!

The 5'7" actress has dealt with comments about her weight and size ever since she started acting — and Kate's not even overweight! "This whole weight thing is nonsense," she says emphatically. "Someone told me the other day that seven out of ten girls under fourteen are watching their weight and skipping meals. That's really scary. It's society, the fashion industry ,and the movie industry. There's so much emphasis on perfect bodies, perfect hair, perfect makeup. . . . No one is perfect. I want to get the message across that these 'perfect bodies' are covered with tons of makeup and hair extensions. In order to be happy and be loved, you don't have to be a size two."

Monica

Matt Damon on Keepin' It Real!

The Oscar-winning actor passes on a tidbit he was given when he first started out as an actor. "You shouldn't take yourself too seriously. I remember when I first got into acting, my agent called one day and said I had a meeting in New York with the head of Walt Disney Studios. I told all my friends about it. When I showed up, I found that it was an audition for the *New Mickey Mouse Club* series. See, it was good that I kept my sense of humor."

Jennifer Aniston

Regis Philbin

The Worst Advice Ever!

Regis Philbin (*Who Wants to be a Millionaire?*): "When I was little, my mother would encourage me to slip under the subway turnstile."

Jennifer Aniston (*Friends*): "I was told to avoid [show] business all together because of the rejection. People would say to me, 'Don't you want to have a normal job and a normal family?' I guess that would be good advice for some people, but I wanted to act."

Claire Danes (*My So-Called Life*): "I was told that my going to college wouldn't be good for my career. I think that's nonsense. It's good to empower yourself by cutting yourself off from the business every once in a while."

Ricky Martin

Be True to Yourself

Full Name: Enrique Jose Martin
Birthdate: December 24, 1971
Birthplace: Santurce, Puerto Rico
Parents: Mother, Nereida Morales; father, Enrique Martin Negroni
Siblings: Brothers, Fernando, Eric, and Daniel; sister, Vanessa
Early Career Goal: To be a singer
First Showbiz Job: Local commercials in Puerto Rico
Career Break: Joined the music group Menudo
Current Job: Pop singer

He's got a dazzling smile, sparkling eyes, not to mention an awesome voice, but Ricky Martin will tell you there are times he's not feeling like Mr. Personality. There are times — especially after being on the road for months, traveling from city to city so often that he doesn't know where he is — that Ricky would rather do anything but smile, talk to people, or deal with the publicity his stardom has created.

But since Ricky has been in show business almost all of his life, he knows the rules. According to him, the first one is: "There's no need to present bad moods when you're in front of the camera."

When Ricky has to let off steam, he does it out of sight of his fans or the cameras. That's a personal thing and he doesn't feel he has to share those emotions with the public. Of course, that's easy to say, and hard to do. As glamorous as his life may seem — limos, champagne, nights on the town — Ricky explains that most times he would rather be home with friends watching TV. The pressures of superstardom are intense. And you can almost feel them when Ricky says, "If I don't have quiet moments when I can just be in touch with my feelings and my emotions, I'll go crazy!"

The Circle of Life

So how does Ricky overcome this push-and-pull existence? First of all, he really does try to lead a normal life when he's back home in Miami. "I try to spend time with my family and friends," he says. "I also meditate, read, listen to music, wash my car, and play with my dogs. I make sure my life is very simple."

Indeed Ricky has found that meditation and the study of yoga has definitely helped him be "grounded and focused. In this business you deal with so much fantasy. . . . the adrenaline is constantly going. I've got to have twenty or forty minutes a day to myself and ask myself how I'm affecting others, how I'm letting others affect me and not be harmed. . . . Meditation is definitely helping. Everybody should try it. It's really good. It helps you get in touch with your body and your mind."

Ricky has actually made several trips to India to visit yoga masters. He has found that this is his personal way of overcoming the obstacles that fame and fortune can present. It has also taught him to deal with the realities of life, too. And it's made him see the irony of seeking stardom and then complaining about it. Says he, "Sometimes it's overwhelming. But if somebody tells you this is a pain in the [butt], smack him in the head! Please, just do it for me!"

How the Stars Overcome Their Personal Obstacles

Taking Control

Alanis Morissette is all about self-awareness and self-esteem in her songs and interviews. She didn't just discover those concepts overnight.

"I had a few boyfriends who . . . took advantage of me. My self-esteem was very low, and I always tried to please everyone, not just boyfriends. I decided the problem wasn't the men, it was me. The moment I let go of trying to please others, I wound up pleasing more people than ever. Being the person you really are solves so many problems."

The Good and the Bad

Comic actress **Janeane Garofalo** had to learn that life isn't always fair.

"In a perfect world, my looks wouldn't make a difference and my self-esteem would be just fine. But that's not the way it works. Before I lost weight, I'd go in for an audition, I'd do a killer job and the casting people would say, 'We love you! We think you're hilarious! But — we're thinking about a different kind of girl.' They were trying to be nice, but it was a big lie. I've learned that if you want your dreams to come true you've just got to be able to take the misses with the hits."

Alanis Morissette

Janeane Garofalo

42

The Darkest Hours

Jewel feels her childhood battle with dyslexia helped make her stronger — especially when she became so knowledgeable about the disorder she actually taught her teachers how to deal with dyslexic students.

"I lost hope when I was ten or eleven. I was doubting myself at that age, I guess that's the darkest. Before that I was a typical girl, dressing up and going, 'Do you like me?'"

Then, when she was fifteen, Jewel was drawn to the study of philosophy and feels it helped her understand herself and focus on her talents, not her shortcomings. "That really changed my whole attitude. It was very empowering. I [was] really shy in my teens. I couldn't move. I was really self-conscious and awkward. By the time I was nineteen, I had gone through so many years of so many phases that I was pretty comfortable with entertaining and getting people going and keeping them interested. . . . I'm shy, but I also love my craft, my job, and I like being good at my job. I've had so many years of getting my brain around that idea from a young age, that by eighteen I was pretty savvy."

Accentuate the Positive

Felicity's **Amy Jo Johnson** recalls her parents were very strict when she was growing up in her small Cape Cod community.

"Kids would make fun of me. It made me feel like an ant. . . . [I went into] a really, really dark depression in seventh and eighth grade. I thought, 'What's the point? We're going to die anyway.'"

Her mother helped pull Amy out of the depression. "She told me to make lists of everything: the things I was grateful for every day. I still do it today . . . Sometimes I think, 'Why did I choose [acting] when I'm so self-conscious?' Every time I go onstage, I say to myself, 'I am doing the wrong thing. I so want to go become a doctor right now.' I cry, I literally cry. And then I'll just find strength deep inside me and end up on a high and be so empowered."

Feeling Good About Yourself

Popular's **Sara Rue (Carmen)** does not exactly fit the stereotypical Hollywood starlet mold: skinny, skinny, skinny, blond, and slightly ditzy. Instead Sara is a size 14, dark haired, and very bright. "I love my body. I think being a woman is wonderful, regardless of size."

When she landed a role in a short-lived series, *Phenom*, Sara and her family moved to Los Angeles. It was 1993, and she recalls, "[We] moved to what I have since learned is truly the land of the thin. A week later, the show was canceled. But I kept going to auditions. I tried to pretend like I was immune to the effects of being surrounded by all these skinny actresses, but I wasn't. I started to play around with diets . . . I knew I was beginning to conform, and I hated that, but I didn't know exactly why. Thinking back, I guess it was because I always had felt good about myself. My parents never made an issue out of my weight while I was growing up, and I never felt the pressure from my managers or agents to lose pounds. Still, I let all the thin images I was inundated with get to me and make me think 'Maybe I should go on a diet.' I would start them all the time, but I never felt right with myself."

Soon Sara found herself being sent only scripts about girls who were miserable about being overweight. Even in her confused state, she knew she didn't want to be typecast that way. Acting was her first love, but she didn't want to use it as way to work out somebody else's idea of the perfect weight. Instead . . .

"I immersed myself in my second love: playing folk music. It's something I picked up from my dad. . . . Rekindling my passion for folk music gave me a safe haven. Once again I became Sara, the self-confident girl I used to be before I allowed the body-conscious hoopla of the entertainment business to toy with my mind. Folk music shifted my focus away from my body and reinforced my confidence in my talent. Before I knew it, my weight seemed like a small issue."

Hold Your Head Up High

Alicia Silverstone could have been overwhelmed by her instant stardom from *Clueless*. And she could have been devastated when her weight became the subject of late-night talk show jokes. She got through both with a lesson she learned years before.

"I've gone through some tough times, like when my whole high school turned on me for no reason. I learned a big lesson that helps me even today: You just have to keep your head up and never let them know they've gotten to you."

Know Your Own Worth

Muhammad Ali has had many highs and lows in his life. He was boxing's Heavyweight Champion three times in his career, but eventually had to battle with Parkinson's disease. Today, Ali remains one of the most respected men in the world. There's a reason: he respects others.

"There are billions of people in the world, and every one of them is special. No one else in the world is like you. Ain't that amazing? Billions of people and every one of them is special."

Jessica Simpson

Write It Down

Full Name: Jessica Ann Simpson

Birthdate: July 10, 1980

Birthplace: Dallas, Texas

Parents: Joe and Tina Simpson

Siblings: Ashlee, 15

Early Career Goal: To Be a Singer

First Showbiz Job: Signed to gospel label at age 13

Career Break: Signed to Columbia Records at age 15

Current Job: Pop singer

When Jessica was fourteen years old, her cousin Sarah was killed in a car accident. It was devastating for Jessica and her tight-knit family. "She was like my best friend," Jessica says as she remembers the times she sat with Sarah and just talked.

However, it wasn't until after Sarah's death that Jessica fully incorporated Sarah's influence in her life. Jessica explains, "Sarah was the one who started me journaling — she always kept a journal. The day of her funeral we all went to her room. Her mother had all her journals laid out where we could look through them. I picked them up and read them. I was so inspired by her words."

Jessica with her boyfriend, Nick Lachey of 98°

Learning to Cope

But it wasn't just Sarah's personal observations that touched Jessica. It was the realization that keeping a journal was a way of dealing with inner turmoil and questions. "All my life any problem I had, [I didn't] deal with it," recalls Jessica. "I pushed [the problem] back further in my mind. I didn't want to deal with it. And when Sarah died, I kept pushing back my feelings of loss. I did not want to deal with it. But when I saw all her writings, I thought 'This is how I have to work through my stuff.'

"So since then, I write down everything. And when I write it down on paper, it's so much easier to deal with because I admit where I'm hurting. [I've realized] pushing things back just makes things worse. But when I write it down, then it's cool. I'll go back to journals I wrote a long time ago, and every prayer I've had has been answered in some way — it's all worked out in some way. It's cool to see the flow of my life."

Animal Actors Have "Tails" Too

7th Heaven's David Gallagher on "Happy"

"During the first season, I was in Ruthie's room. We had this big pterodactyl kite hung up in the corner of the room, and Happy had to be on the bunk bed. One of the grip guys was behind the wall hammering something and the pterodactyl fell down and almost hit Happy. Happy jumped out of her fur — and off the bunk bed. She took a flying leap into someone's arms. She was shaking and we couldn't get her to do anything she was so scared. . . . Happy's scared of heights — she hates being up on the bunk bed. But, I mean, she took a flying leap!"

David and Happy

Animorphs Stars on Their "Alter Egos"

Shawn Ashmore: "Animals being animals — and wild animals at that — you don't know what they're going to do. The lions mark their territory by peeing backwards. They can spray twenty feet and if you get it on your clothes, you'll never get it out. It has definitely happened a couple of times. Luckily, I've never been on the receiving end of the lion's gift!"

Christopher Ralph: "[My first animal-morph was the] hawk. Well, the hawk, whenever we're shooting, he has a tendency to relieve himself — during the takes!"

Nadia Nascimento: "Weird things happen with the animals. It's always fun when Bongo the lion comes because we know something's going to happen. He makes us laugh because he's smart. During every rehearsal — we have to rehearse with the lion just so he'll do things properly, and won't start charging and eating all the directors. So, when we rehearse, he nails it every time. Then the second we say, 'Roll film,' I think he laughs and says to himself 'I'm going to screw them up!' So every time they roll the camera, Bongo goes the other way or he sprays someone!"

ENRE ❷ HB